IN SEARCH OF
TROY

Piero Ventura and Gian Paolo Ceserani

Silver Burdett Company
Morristown, New Jersey

In Search of Troy
Copyright © Arnoldo Mondadori Editore S.p.A.,
Milan
Translated from the Italian by Pamela Swinglehurst
Editor: Philip Steele
Design: Sally Boothroyd

First published in Great Britain in 1985 by
Macdonald & Co. (Publishers) Ltd
London & Sydney

Adapted and published in the United States in 1985 by
Silver Burdett Company, Morristown, New Jersey

Printed and bound in Spain
by Artes Graficas Toledo S.A.
D. L. TO:1857 -1987

Note: much argument and controversy still surround the story of
Heinrich Schliemann. In some instances the artist and author have
given their impressions and own interpretation of what *may* have
happened. Sadly, "Priam's Treasure" was stolen from its museum in
Germany after the Second World War. The most modern dating
methods cannot therefore be applied. So, controversy will no doubt
continue to surround its discovery.

Library of Congress Cataloging in Publication Data
Ventura, Piero.
  In search of Troy.

  Summary: Traces Heinrich Schliemann's search for and
discovery of the site of ancient Troy and discusses
the mythology and possible historical facts connected
with the siege of that city.
  1. Troy (Ancient city) – Juvenile literature.
2. Schliemann, Heinrich, 1822-1890 – Juvenile literature.
[1. Troy (Ancient city) 2. Schliemann, Heinrich, 1822-
1890. 3. Mythology, Greek] I. Ceserani, Gian Paolo,
1939- . II. Title III. Title: Troy.
DF221.T8V44 1985   939.21   85-40415

ISBN 0-382-09121-3 (soft)
ISBN 0-382-09118-3 (lib. bdg.)

Contents

Corfu

GREECE

Mt Olympus

Ithaca

Cephalonia

Xanthe

Olympia

Corinth

Athens

Mycenae

Argos

Ionian Sea

Sparta

O Troy

TURKEY

Lesbos

Aegean Sea

Chios

Samos

Naxos

Rhodes

Dreams of Troy

One of the most exciting stories ever told is called the *Iliad*. It was probably composed by a Greek poet called Homer sometime around 850 BC. It tells the story of a city called Troy, which was besieged and burned down by the ancient Greeks.

The story was written so long ago that we no longer know very much about the author, or indeed about the city of Troy. Like all good stories it was passed down from one generation to the next. Some storytellers would change the plot here and there, and invent new details. How much of the story as we know it today was really true? We do not know.

People had been arguing about Homer for hundreds of years. Some of them said that the *Iliad* was not written by Homer at all. Some said that the story was not true either, that the poet had simply made up an exciting tale. One man did not agree. He was called Heinrich Schliemann.

Heinrich Schliemann was a wealthy German businessman. He traveled to many parts of the world and he taught himself no less than 18 foreign

Schliemann's birthplace

Amsterdam

languages. Having become rich, he decided to spend his time and money on studying ancient history and archaeology. Schliemann was sure that ancient Troy really did exist – and he set out to find it.

To everyone's surprise it turned out that Schliemann was no rich fool or idle dreamer. He excavated in Greece at Mycenae, Ithaca, Orchomenos, and Tiryns – and at Hissarlik, in the country now known as Turkey. It was Schliemann's dig at Hissarlik which was to first astound the world. Here he uncovered the remains of a very ancient city. Could it be that a mere amateur archaeologist had discovered the Troy of Homer? Who was this man?

Heinrich Schliemann was born on January 6, 1822, in the Mecklenburg region of northern Germany. His father was a protestant pastor. Schliemann claimed that much of his childhood was spent dreaming of the ghosts which were said to haunt the neighborhood!

His interest in ancient history came from his father. From him Schliemann first heard of the lost cities of the ancient world. He heard of Herculaneum and Pompeii, the Roman towns which lay buried for 17 centuries. He read the *Iliad* and was fascinated by the great walled city of Troy and the tale of its destruction.

Schliemann's family went through hard times. He had to give up his studies and start to earn his living. At the age of 18 we find him in Amsterdam, the capital of the Netherlands.

He worked as an errand boy and was excited by the hustle and bustle of the big city. Amsterdam was an important center of world trade, and young Heinrich dreamed of traveling to distant countries.

He decided to seek his fortune, and found a ship sailing for South America. He never even reached the Atlantic: the ship sank in the English Channel. Schliemann swam ashore to the island of Texel and made his way back to Amsterdam. He worked hard, and soon his employers gave him the chance he had been waiting for. He was to become their representative in the Russian city of St Petersburg – now known as Leningrad.

9

St Petersburg in 1846

The Russian trader

Heinrich Schliemann arrived in the frost and snow of St Petersburg in January, 1846. In those days Russia was ruled by the tsars, and St Petersburg was the royal capital. It was a busy town. The young businessman settled down to a life of hard work.

Schliemann imported goods such as sugar, coffee, and indigo from tropical countries. Indigo is a plant used to make a deep blue dye; today we use chemicals instead. Schliemann was determined to be successful. Like many people in the Victorian period, he worked tirelessly. He spared nobody, least of all himself.

Schliemann had little time for leisure. When he did allow himself some free time, he used it to learn languages. He approached his studies with the same spirit with which he tackled his work. He soon found that he could learn any language thoroughly within a few months.

Schliemann worked out his own system of learning. He would read aloud a lot, without translating, and write essays. He had a daily lesson, at which the teacher would correct his essays. He would then learn the corrections off by heart.

Schliemann was able to concentrate on his learning at any moment of the day. Even standing in a post office line he would be memorizing his studies. Schliemann did not think he was very good at languages, but he soon spoke many fluently.

It was clear that Heinrich Schliemann was a very able man, with a great deal of will power. He was successful at his business and was wealthy before he reached his 30th birthday. But he was a dreamer too, and was beginning to grow weary of St Petersburg.

His interest turned again to the Americas.
He had a brother named Ludwig in California. When Ludwig died, Heinrich decided to sail to the United States to settle his brother's estate.

Once again Schliemann's ship was to sink, and he found himself back in Europe. He was not a man to be put off easily. Within a week he was back at sea! This time his ship, the *Africa*, crossed to New York without any problem.

American adventure

Having arrived in New York City, Heinrich Schliemann set out to explore this exciting new country. He was impressed by the size of the buildings in New York, and traveled south to Philadelphia and Baltimore. In Washington, DC, he visited the Capitol building, the home of the United States government. He even met President Fillmore and his family.

Schliemann took detailed notes during his travels. Like many rich people, he was very careful with his money. He noted down the prices of everything. A night in a New York hotel cost two dollars and fifty cents, for example. Wine was extra.

It was time for Schliemann to move on to California. In those days of course there were no cars or buses, and no planes. Railways were only just beginning to appear. The journey across

America was long and hard. Schliemann decided to sail south to the Isthmus of Panama. He sailed up the Pacific Coast and arrived in San Francisco.

Heinrich Schliemann was fascinated by San Francisco. Only 18 months before it had been little more than a village. Now it had a population of 40,000, and there were some 800 ships anchored in the Bay. The houses and raised pavements (known as "sidewalks") were made of wooden planks.

Heinrich Schliemann now had to visit Sacramento, where his brother Ludwig had made his home. Schliemann loved traveling through this wild, beautiful countryside. Sacramento was a town of 10,000 people. It had so much open, green space, that it was possible to hunt rabbits, quail and even coyotes in the middle of town! Schliemann settled his brother's affairs and ordered a tombstone in his memory. He decided to make Sacramento his home as well.

Schliemann returned briefly to San Francisco. It was the evening of June 3, 1851. He checked into the Plaza Hotel. No sooner was he asleep than he was awakened by an alarm bell and the sound of screaming. The city was on fire.

Schliemann got up, threw on some clothes and ran down the street. A few minutes later the hotel was in flames. Wind fanned the burning buildings, and the wooden city was ablaze. Even brick houses were falling down. Houses built around iron frames were glowing and showering sparks into the sky.

Schliemann made his way through the fleeing crowds to Telegraph Hill. The scene was frightening. A red glow lit up the roofs and walls of the city. Every so often there would be a loud crash or an explosion. People huddled together and comforted crying children. They collected together the few possessions they had managed to save from the flames. Schliemann could never forget the terrible sight.

The wild west

The day after the great fire, the people of San Francisco began to clear up the damage. Schliemann watched them.

He noticed that the foreigners, the British, French and Germans, sat weeping over their misfortunes. The Americans, however, set about rebuilding their city. This was what Schliemann liked about America. The people were active, tough, and cheerful. He saw the United States as his new homeland.

There was one thing Schliemann did not like in America: the love of money. Although he had himself become a wealthy businessman, he had many *other* interests in life.

These were the years of the Gold Rush. The precious metal had been discovered in California. Thousands of people from the eastern states and from Europe made the dangerous journey westwards across America. They came to find gold and seek their fortune. Very few found it.

The people who did become rich were businessmen like Heinrich Schliemann. He opened a bank in Sacramento. Business was good. It was helped by the fact that Schliemann could speak so many different languages with his customers!

Not everything went well for Schliemann. The climate was unhealthy. Many people in Sacramento had malaria and dysentery. Schliemann caught a fever and very nearly died. He was sent to the healthier town of San José to recover. He was a strong man and was soon back at work.

Schliemann's life was certainly more adventurous than that of most businessmen. One night there was a terrible flood in Sacramento. There was a dam on the river and part of it burst.

Hundreds of men struggled to repair the damage, but then a whole section of the dam gave way. Men were hurled into the water, and Schliemann himself was battered and bruised. The waters of the river swept into town. Soon they were swirling around the buildings, about twelve feet deep. People scrambled to the rooftops for safety.

Yet again, the Americans coped with the disaster admirably. They built rafts, rowed around in empty barrels, and made money by ferrying people to and fro. Luckily for Schliemann, his bank was not flooded and the money was safe.

Much as Schliemann enjoyed life in America, he did miss Europe. After less than a year he decided to return home. In April, 1852, he set out for the Isthmus of Panama, where he had further adventures. It was August before he arrived back in St Petersburg.

He was now 30 years old, successful and rich. However, his travels had changed him a lot. He continued to work hard, but he longed for a change. He had made enough money to live off comfortably. What should he do now?

His first thought was to learn another language: Greek. He had always longed to study Greek, but had been afraid that it would take up too much of his precious time. Now he had time.

Schliemann learned modern Greek in six weeks, following his own method. He then tackled ancient Greek. Within three months he was able to read the *Iliad* in Greek. He then read the *Odyssey*, the story of Ulysses, which was also thought to have been composed by Homer.

For two years Schliemann did little but pore over the texts of these two books. Finally he decided to finish with the world of business once and for all. He would devote the rest of his life to travel and study.

The island of Ulysses

In 1858 and 1859 Heinrich Schliemann visited Jerusalem, Damascus and Athens. He traveled to Italy and Egypt, where he learned Arabic. He then went on a tour of the world, visiting North Africa, Japan, and India. He saw Malta, Pompeii and Paestum. Once again he crossed the Atlantic, to visit the United States, Canada, Mexico, and Cuba.

He never stayed anywhere very long. He had become a restless person. The more he traveled, the more he realized that he had a lot to learn.

In February, 1866, Heinrich Schliemann took a course of study at the Sorbonne, in Paris, a very famous university. He studied languages and literature. To the young students he must have seemed quite an old fellow. He was 44 years old, and gray-haired.

That summer Schliemann visited Ithaca, a beautiful island off the western coast of Greece. It was an important moment for the German traveler. According to legend, this was the home of Ulysses, the hero of the *Odyssey*. It was from Ithaca that Ulysses was said to have sailed off to fight the Trojans.

Schliemann explored the island. He had read so much Homer that he now believed every word to be true. He used the *Odyssey* as his guide book to Ithaca. He declared that he had even found the spot where Ulysses' dog Argus had died!

Every hill and valley meant something to him. It really was wishful thinking and nobody could believe him.

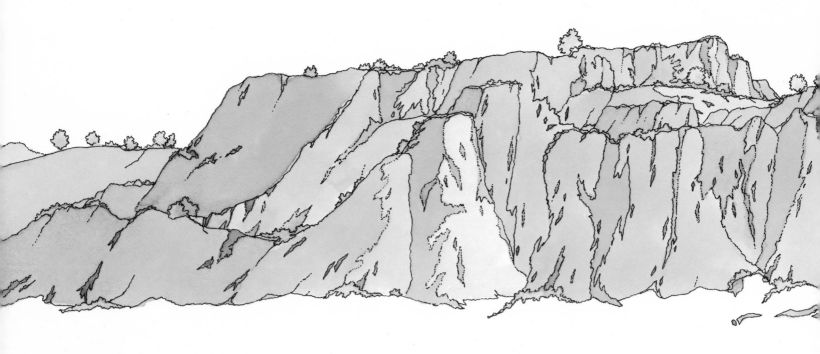

Hissarlik

Heinrich Schliemann believed in Homer. Why did no one believe in Heinrich Schliemann? The problem was this: nobody knew anything about Homer. There were no historical records of the poet at all. Who was he? Where had he lived? When had he lived?

If he had existed it must have been sometime around 850 BC. But the Trojan War probably took place in the 11th or 12th century BC – three or four hundred years earlier. Schliemann thought that writing was not used at the time of the Trojan War. In fact it was. So the story may have been written down as well as passed on from one storyteller to another.

You could hardly blame the archaeologists of Schliemann's day for not taking his theories seriously. What about today? Now that we have found out so much more about history, can we agree with Schliemann?

Not really. The works of Homer cannot be seen as any kind of historical record or accurate account of the Trojan War. However there is clearly *some* truth in it. Homer describes the Mycenaeans. We now know that a great civilization *did* exist at Mycenae at the time of the Trojan War. Mycenaeans could read and write, and their way of life must have been much as it was described by Homer.

Today we think that it is more than likely that Homer really did exist. He was probably the author of the *Iliad*, and possibly of the *Odyssey*, although that might have been written at a later date. In the *Iliad* Homer sometimes describes the dress and customs of his own day. However, his picture of Greece as a whole is probably much the same as it

was during the Trojan War.

Homer describes a number of cities and kingdoms which really existed. We know that these kingdoms often formed alliances and fought against each other, just as Homer describes. We know that Troy was a real city on the coast of what is now called Turkey. The wealth of the city was based on trading. Of course the Greeks would have made war on this powerful rival.

So Schliemann was not exactly right – but then he was not exactly wrong. The ancient Greeks themselves had had few doubts about Homer. They were sure he had really existed and that he had actually invented the kind of poetry used in the *Iliad*. The Greek historian Thucydides, who lived in the 5th century BC, thought that Homer had written a poetic, but basically true account of the Trojan War.

One question was worrying Heinrich Schliemann. The more he read of the *Iliad* the more he worried about it. *Where* was Troy? If only he could find the site of the ancient city.

In ancient times the *Iliad* had been read by many famous soldiers, such as Xerxes, Alexander the Great, and Julius Caesar. They all agreed where the city had once stood – on a hill known in modern times as Hissarlik. In Schliemann's day many people disagreed with this theory. They believed Bali Dagh was the site of Troy.

Schliemann could wait no longer. He visited Bali Dagh, and checked it against the description of Troy in the *Iliad*. It was too different. The plain in front of the sea was too long, and the sea was too far away.

He traveled on to Hissarlik. As he stared across the dusty plain at the rocky hill, he was sure that he was looking at the site of ancient Troy.

The excavation

Heinrich Schliemann paced around Hissarlik, mopping his brow. He had a copy of the *Iliad* in his hand. This rocky plateau must have been the site of the walled city. That was the coast where the Greek ships had been beached. There was the plain where they had camped and fought.

Schliemann made some calculations. The city walls must have been about three miles long. In the *Iliad* a fight is described between the warriors Hector and Achilles. They are said to have chased each other around the city three times. That would be nine miles – a reasonable distance for war chariots.

Here too was a chain of mountains, just as they were described by Homer...there was the peak of Mount Ida. There was no doubt in his mind. On April 9, 1870, Heinrich Schliemann began the excavation of Hissarlik. Workers with pickaxes started delving into the secrets of the hillside.

A palace and a temple were soon uncovered. Schliemann was thrilled. He had checked the *Iliad*. The highest point of the city had been the temple of the goddess Athene, according to Homer. The lowest point had been the fortress of King Priam.

In those days people knew little about archaeology. Sometimes they were careless and did not record things properly. Schliemann made some very bad mistakes. He decided to dig a broad trench across the hill from north to south. Everything in its path was damaged or destroyed, and no records were made.

Schliemann did not understand something that every archaeologist must learn. Important sites have often been occupied by humans over many thousands of years. New cities are built on the ruins of old ones. In any excavation the oldest layers are obviously the deepest.

Schliemann dug down relentlessly, and uncovered a city that was as much as a thousand years earlier than the one he had been looking for! In the process, he destroyed a large part of the Troy he was seeking.

Another lesson any archaeologist must learn is this: make sure that permission has been granted for excavation of the site in question. Quite understandably, the peasants who owned the land around Hissarlik complained to the Turkish authorities. In the end, Schliemann had to apply for a permit.

He was not a patient man. Hours and hours were spent in government offices, writing, arguing and appealing. Needless to say, the waiting hours were spent learning the Turkish language. At last the permit was issued. Work could proceed.

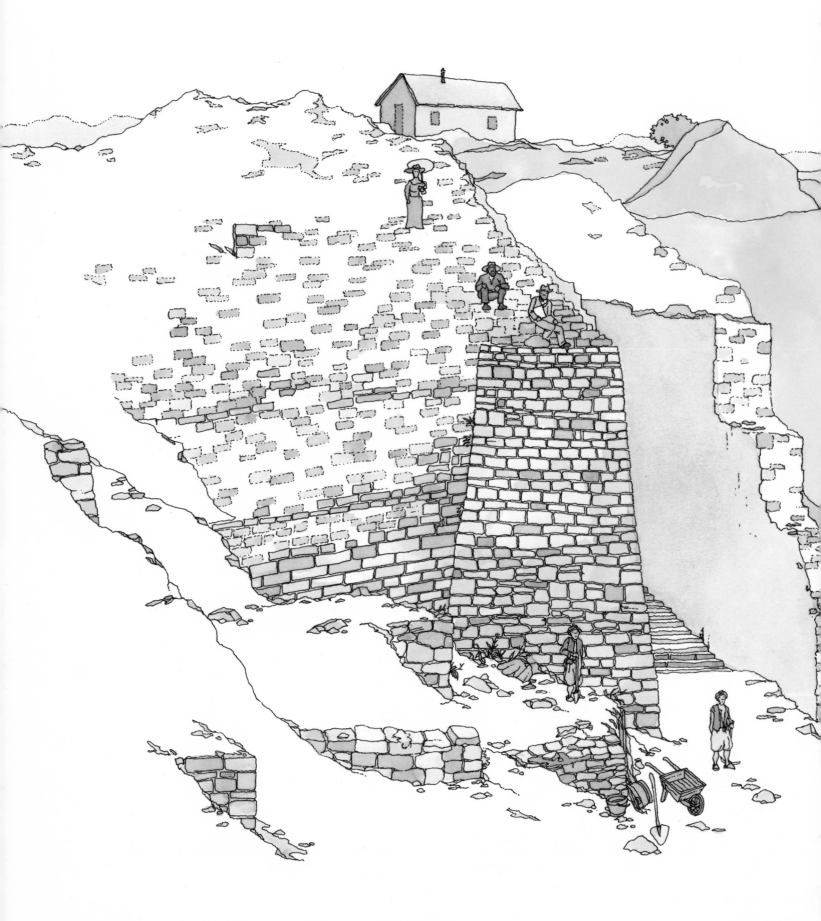

The walls of Troy

Heinrich Schliemann had remarried in 1869. His wife was a beautiful young Greek girl called Sophie. The marriage was a happy one, and Schliemann bought a house in Athens, the capital of Greece. There, he felt at home.

On the site at Hissarlik, Schliemann missed the comforts of home. Here amidst the dust and rocks there were insects, parasites, scorpions and millipedes. There were tiny poisonous snakes, and at night the hooting of owls kept him awake.

The heat was stifling, and Hissarlik was far from any town. The site was often chaotic.

He continued to argue with the Turkish officials. He was thankful for his wife's company and support. Sophie was a hardy traveler and kept Schliemann from despairing.

The news of Heinrich Schliemann's discoveries spread around the world from Turkey. He sent articles to English and German newspapers, and these aroused a great deal of interest with the public. He was however ignored by the scientists and the big museums. They did not think that this amateur would make any great discoveries.

They were wrong. In 1873 Schliemann's fortunes improved. He found further city walls, an altar that had been used for sacrifices, and a paved road. A palace was uncovered, which Schliemann was sure was that of ancient Troy.

And then Schliemann made a discovery which astounded the world: a hoard of precious objects. Could this be the treasure of King Priam? Nobody could ignore Schliemann any longer.

King Priam's treasure?

Schliemann himself described in a book how he discovered "Priam's treasure." He was digging in a layer of red ash and rubble about five feet deep. Suddenly his pick struck a copper object. He immediately gave the order for the workers to take a break. This could be a valuable discovery, and secrecy was the best policy.

A breathtaking series of treasures came to light. First there was a shield, about a foot and a half long. Then there was a basin, plate, and vase of copper. Next there appeared a goblet of pure gold, and then another shaped like a ship. There followed jewels, diadems, necklaces, bracelets of gold and silver.

Schliemann scraped at the precious objects with his knife. Sophie wrapped them in her shawl and carried them to safety. Later she was to try on the jewelry: she looked like a queen. Heinrich Schliemann claimed that he was certain that this was the treasure of Priam.

We know now of course that Schliemann was digging at a deeper level than he should have been. The objects he found were some thousand years older than the age of Priam. Far from solving the riddle of Troy once and for all, Schliemann simply left us more questions to answer. Who had made the treasure? Had it been manufactured in Troy at all? Did Schliemann really find it all in a great hoard?

This was to be a problem for modern archaeologists to tackle. Whatever mistakes Schliemann did make, we must give him credit for persistence and for recognizing the drama and romance of discovery.

Schliemann was a restless man, and as full of energy as ever. In 1876 he started excavating another site mentioned in the *Iliad*: Mycenae, in Greece. Yet again, he unearthed fabulous treasures.

These, he claimed, were from the age of Agamemnon, King of Mycenae at the time of the Trojan War. Again he was wrong: the treasure was about four hundred years older than he thought. Nevertheless, it was magnificent.

Schliemann's fame spread throughout the world. Even the experts had to make their peace with him. In 1889 Schliemann proudly received the leading scholars of the day at the Hissarlik site. He still had many critics, but his achievements were recognized at last.

In 1890 Heinrich Schliemann decided to visit the excavations at Pompeii, in southern Italy. While in Naples, on December 26, he died. Schliemann had led an extraordinary life of adventure.

His successes had been won through sheer hard work.

Despite the mistakes he made, we owe a great deal to this German businessman. The results of his work were spectacular. Yet, perhaps, just as valuable was the way in which he changed people's view of the ancient world.

A hundred years ago people had no idea that civilization stretched back for thousands of years. Schliemann awakened people's imagination, and passed on to them his own enthusiasm.

King Priam's treasure

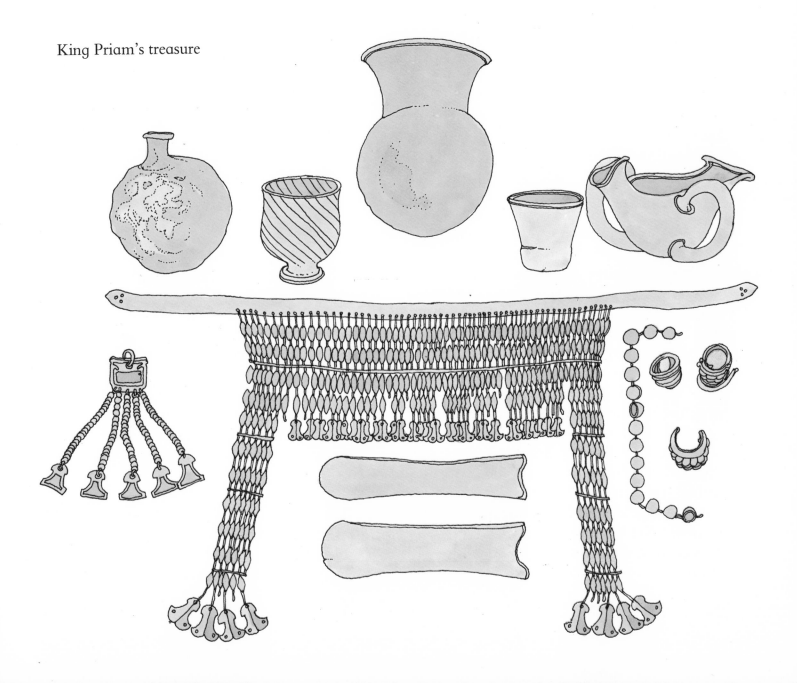

The cities on the hill

Heinrich Schliemann had completed his work. It was now up to historians and archaeologists to piece together a picture of ancient Troy.

Today we know much more about accurate dating than we did in Schliemann's day. For example, we know that the biblical city of Jericho, and Katal Huyük in Turkey, date from 7000 BC and 6000 BC. There were probably cities on the hill of Hissarlik from 3000 BC to AD 400.

Archaeologists have worked out that there must have been no less than nine different settlements on the hill at different points in history.

The first city of Troy belongs to the earliest Bronze Age. It had thick walls, towers, and wide gates; it was destroyed by fire. From its ruins arose the second city of Troy, which had four gates and towers which projected over the walls.

The ages passed. Cities would be destroyed by fire or earthquake, and new walls would be raised. It is probably the seventh settlement of Hissarlik which is the Troy of the *Iliad*. It seems to have been burned down around the middle of the 13th century BC.

What was this city like? How was it built? It had massive walls, gates and towers. The royal palace stood at the highest point, with the houses spreading down the hillside. Only about 3,000 people would have lived there.

The walls of the city and the palace were built with stones and rocks, but most of the houses were very simple. For them, clay bricks were used which had been baked in the sun. The walls were strengthened with wooden beams and the roofs were covered with reeds.

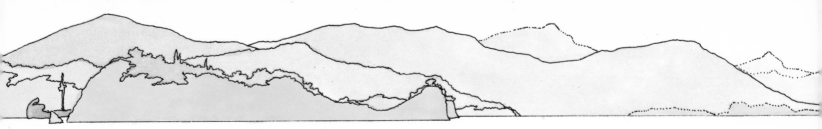

Goddesses and heroes

How did people live in the 13th century BC? It was Homer's *Iliad* which made Heinrich Schliemann interested in ancient Troy. We could do worse than follow his example, and turn to the famous story of the Trojan War. Unlike Schliemann, we know that we must not take the story too literally...

The *Iliad* is written in a style of poetry that we call "epic." This means that it describes acts of bravery, heroic deeds and great tragedies. The book is made up of individual episodes, such as a fight between two warriors. Storytellers have always loved telling tales like these.

When Homer starts his tale, the Greeks have been at war with Troy for ten long years. There have been many battles, but neither side is the overall winner. Why did the Greeks ever leave their homeland and sail across the Aegean Sea?

The ancient Greeks believed in many different gods and goddesses. They told many stories about them, and to us their gods often seem more like human beings. Homer blames the start of the Trojan War on three goddesses.

According to the poet, King Priam of Troy has a son called Paris. Paris is asked to decide which of the three goddesses is the most beautiful: Hera, Aphrodite, or Athene. He chooses Aphrodite. In return for the favor, she helps Paris carry off the wife of Menelaus, King of Sparta. Her name is Helen, and she is very beautiful. Menelaus and the other Greek leaders declare war on Troy, to regain their honor and recapture the lovely Helen.

So much for the story. What really happened? The war was probably fought over trade. Troy was a wealthy city. Ships sailed from her shores laden with valuable textiles. The Greek kingdoms too, traded in woolen goods. They presumably decided to stop fighting each other and to form an alliance. Their aim: to destroy their common rival, Troy.

If for a moment we ignore the gods and goddesses, we see the Greeks as they must have been: a warlike, seafaring people. Their ships, waterproofed with black pitch, sailed back and forth across the sparkling blue waters of the Aegean Sea. They traded and formed raiding parties; they were brave, cunning, argumentative, but heroic.

The warrior kings

No epic poem of ancient times was complete without a long list of names. They give us many clues about ancient Greece. While Homer exaggerates the brave deeds of his heroes, he is always very precise about where they come from.

Agamemnon is King of Mycenae, the most powerful of the Greek kingdoms at that time. His brother is Menelaus, the King of Sparta. Achilles, the bravest of all the warriors in the *Iliad*, is King of the Myrmidons of Thessaly. Diomedes is King of Argos.

The brave Ajax is the son of Telemon, from the island kindgom of Salamis. Another warrior called Ajax is the son of Oileus, King of the Locrians. Nestor is King of Pylos in Messenia. Ulysses, the

chief character of the *Odyssey*, is the King of Ithaca – the very island from which Heinrich Schliemann started his quest.

There seem to have been many kings in one small part of the world! In reality many of these would have been the rulers of small islands and towns. Few people lived in Greece in this period. It was a small world in which individual characters stood out.

One kingdom which was very powerful was Mycenae. Thanks to Schliemann's excavations we know that Mycenae was a great kingdom as early as 1400 BC. Homer tells us of its city's massive walls and wide streets, its fine buildings and its riches. We now know the details of this city: its fortifications, its bridges and aqueducts. The Mycenaeans occupied some other Greek states such as Sparta, and attacked lands to the east. Mycenae would have been the chief rival of Troy.

The splendors of the age of Mycenae were soon forgotten. Centuries later, when Homer was writing the *Iliad*, they were only a distant memory.

Let us return to the story of the *Iliad*. The Greeks are camped in front of the city of Troy. The hill of Hissarlik was once by the sea, at the point where two rivers joined together, the Scamander and the Simois. The plain which

Schliemann walked over was created when these two rivers silted up. Whether the Greeks originally landed here or farther south is a matter of argument among scholars.

The camp of the Greeks is in a state of despair. A deadly plague has broken out, and many of their comrades have died. Their bodies are burned on funeral pyres, and a pall of black smoke hangs over the shore. The Greeks ask Calchas, a soothsayer, to explain their misfortunes.

He says they are being punished by the god Apollo. Agamemnon has seized the daughter of the priest of Apollo. If the plague is to end, Agamemnon must return the girl to her father.

As the King of Mycenae, Agamemnon is the most powerful of the warrior kings. He is angry at the suggestion that he has been the cause of the disaster. He says he will only give the girl back if he can have another one – a slave girl belonging to Achilles. Achilles is of course furious at this arrogant behavior.

Reading between the lines of the *Iliad* we can get some idea of the realities of war in ancient times. The warriors were at the end of a ten-year long campaign. They were battle-weary and homesick. Disease was common in these unhealthy spots, and tempers were wearing thin.

The skirmish

Achilles has had enough. He and his men refuse to fight the Trojans any more. Discontent spreads among the Greeks, and soon there is talk of sailing for home.

Arguments and mutinies must have been common among the Greeks. Remember that they were not a single nation, but a federation of communities. They were more used to fighting each other than the enemy. The Trojan forces also relied on allied troops.

If we follow the *Iliad* we see the continuing battles between the Trojans and the Greeks as a series of single combats. The warrior seizes his chariot, races towards the enemy, and then dismounts to fight on foot.

The reality must have been rather different. The chariots must have been used in wider maneuvers, and the troops must have fought in line.

And yet the spirit of Homer rings true. The warriors would challenge each other and exchange insults or grudging praise as they skirmished in the dust.

City under siege

What of the warriors of Troy? The chief hero is Hector, the son of Priam. Homer shows him to us as he meets his wife Andromache at the Scaean Gate. Below him the plain is filled with fighting men. We see him torn between the war and his love for his wife and his baby son Astyanax. He then mounts his chariot and rides to battle – outside the city walls.

When we read of a siege we tend to think of the way in which castles were besieged in medieval Europe. There the city would be completely cut off by the enemy.

Homer's account of the siege of Troy is rather different. He describes no shortage of food and water. The Greeks do not use battering rams, or make ladders to scale the city walls.

It is possible that the siege of Troy was a series of attacks and counterattacks rather than a proper siege. What town could have survived ten years of total siege?

Perhaps the Greeks would appear in their ships, set up camp and fight for a few months. They would then withdraw for a period, only to reappear at the gates of Troy the following season. The Trojans would sally forth in pursuit, and then the fighting would begin again.

The buildings of Troy would have remained unharmed by most of the fighting on the plains below. Homer mentions Priam's splendid palace with 50 rooms for his 50 sons; the *agora*, where the citizens of Troy met in assembly; the temples of Athene and Apollo; and the grand houses of Hector and Paris.

Troy was a city of the Bronze Age. Homer describes an incident in which the Trojan warrior Glaucus exchanges armor with the Greek Diomedes. Glaucus' armor is made of gold, and is said to be worth a hundred oxen. Diomedes' armor is made of bronze, and worth only nine oxen.

Coins were not used for money in Troy. Silver, barley, or oxen were the normal currency. The *Iliad* tells us that a slave girl was worth four oxen, and that a tripod – a basin supported by three legs – was worth twelve.

Exchanges and gifts were very important in the ancient world. Deals were made between men which would bind them together for the rest of their lives – and sometimes their descendants, too. A person's standing was measured by the amount of valuable objects he or she possessed.

The Trojans

To an archaeologist, 3000 years is not really such a long time. We know a great deal about life in ancient Egypt for example. But Schliemann's excavation has given a few clues about everyday life in ancient Troy. We must make a guess, relying on our knowledge of other cities of the period.

The Trojans were traders, producing textiles and other craft work. They owned flocks of sheep, which produced the yarn for weaving. They probably had linen garments as well as woolen, made from flax.

Crops probably included wheat and barley and various vegetables. They grew beans, chick peas, and lentils. They had no sugar, of course, using honey for sweetening food.

What would a Trojan have eaten for a meal? Olives, bread, oil, cheese and milk provided by sheep and goats, and vegetables. They ate very little fruit, except for grapes and figs. Their herds and flocks provided meat, which could be washed down with wine.

The produce of the craft workers was very important. The story of Glaucus' armor confirms that Troy was rich in gold. Some craft workers were skilled with gold, others with silver and bronze.

wine making

chariot building

weaving

a potter's wheel

Others were blacksmiths, potters, chariot makers, leather workers, and - above all - weavers.

As in many ancient societies, people preferred to own precious objects that could easily be carried in the event of war, plague, fire, earthquake, or any other of the disasters which were all too common in those days.

Horses were very important to the Trojans. Homer calls Hector "The Tamer of Horses." Horses were bred for use in war chariots. Like the Greeks, the Trojans must have been good sailors. They would carry sheep and horses by boat, which is no easy matter.

Although the Trojans were traders, we do not know whether they traveled far to sell their goods. Perhaps they sold to the Phoenicians, the famous traders of the Mediterranean, rather than directly to other cities.

The Greek camp

The Greeks had to protect themselves from counterattack. Their ships were beached and they depended on the fleet for their survival. They therefore built a long turf rampart around their camp.

This camp would have been well guarded. Instead of tents, Homer tells us that the Greeks erected huts, where they rested from battle. Perhaps this was because the war had gone on for so long. Certainly if the Greek troops were fighting all the year round, they would need shelter: the climate around Hissarlik can be bitterly cold in the winter months.

If we return to Homer's account of the fighting, we find the Greek camp is under attack. The Trojans have heard of the quarrel between Agamemnon and Achilles. This seems to be the ideal time for a sally.

Trojan chariots stream out from the city walls, and their warriors swarm over the ramparts. Soon the camp is ablaze, and the Greeks are pressed back to their ships. Agamemnon sends a desperate plea to Achilles. But no help comes.

Fight to the death

Homer's story now takes a new turn. Achilles is at last persuaded to let his friend Patroclus fight on his behalf, wearing his armor.

The Greeks rally around Patroclus and force the Trojans out of their camp. In the thick of the fighting, however, Patroclus is cut down by Hector, the great Trojan warrior. Around the body, men are fighting for the armor: arms were always a valuable prize of battle.

At last Achilles is moved to fight. In a high rage he arms himself and rides to battle to avenge his dead friend Patroclus. The Trojans flee in terror and are soon back beneath their own city walls.

Here the two great heroes meet in combat for the last time. Hector is completely unnerved by the battle-fury of Achilles, and he flees. Three times he is chased around the walls of the city. At last, exhausted, he turns to fight.

Achilles throws his spear, but misses. Hector hurls his spear at the Greek, but it is turned away by the shield. He draws his sword and rushes upon Achilles - but the Greek has his spear back, and pierces Hector through the throat.

The Trojan champion lies bleeding to death in the dust. Achilles shows no mercy. He is still in a mad rage. With contempt, he strips off Hector's armor and lets the Greeks stab at the body. Achilles then strings Hector's body to his chariot. He gallops around the city walls, dragging the corpse through the dust.

The story is a brutal one, but it does give a true picture of the horrors of war.

The gods were, of course, very important to the ancient Greeks, and Homer always explains away the events that happen by referring to them.

According to Homer, Achilles was such a great warrior because his mother was the goddess Thetis. His shield stopped Hector's spear because it had been made by Hephaestus, the master-smith of the gods. Achilles could not be injured because his mother had dipped him as a baby in the magic waters of the River Styx.

Yet even the gods made mistakes. When Thetis bathed Achilles in the Styx, she held him by the heel. This is his one weak spot, and it causes his death. Achilles is finally struck in the heel by an arrow fired by the Trojan prince Paris. Paris was the handsome coward who had stolen Helen from Menelaus, and so started the Trojan War in the first place.

The games

One of the most interesting parts of the *Iliad* is not about the fighting at all, and the Trojans play no part in it. At the funeral of Patroclus, games are held in his honor.

Homer tells about the competition at some length. He is rather like a modern sports commentator. Every detail of the contest is recorded, even the advice which is passed on to the athletes by the spectators.

Why is this so interesting? Because it describes an early version of the sporting contests so popular with the ancient Greeks, the most famous of which was to become the Olympic Games.

Homer lists the prizes for the winners. There are horses, oxen, and mules. There are slaves. There is gold, and bowls and basins of silver. There is "gray iron." This must have been meteorite iron, as precious as jewels during the Bronze Age.

Eight events take place: chariot racing, boxing, wrestling, running, single combat, archery, throwing the discus and the javelin.

The most famous warriors of all take part in the funeral games: Agamemnon, Ulysses, Diomedes, Ajax son of Telemon, and Menelaus, the husband of Helen. Homer adds in the names of other famous sportsmen, whose names have not yet appeared in the story: Epeius the boxer, Polypoetes the discus thrower, Teucer and Meriones the archers.

The Mycenaeans are thought to have started the custom of the games. Historians believe the first true Olympic Games were held in 776 BC. Olympia was a site in southern Greece. Here there were shrines, temples, and stadiums. The ruins of Olympia still stand today.

The Olympic Games were held every four years, and lasted for five days. Greeks would come from every part of the country to Olympia. All wars and disputes between the Greek states would be suspended and the athletes would train at home for ten months. The winners received great honors. The Olympic Games came to an end in AD 394; they were revived in Athens in 1896 and are still held today.

chariot racing

wrestling

archery

running

boxing

single combat

throwing the discus

The wooden horse

Homer does not finish the story of Troy in the *Iliad*. He ends the tale at the point where the King of Troy, Priam, goes to Achilles to ask for the body of his son, Hector.

Achilles is moved by the old man's courage and dignity. He returns the battered body to the Trojans, and the *Iliad* ends with the funeral of Hector.

If, however, we leave the *Iliad*, we find that the story carries on in other books. In the *Odyssey* we follow the wanderings of Ulysses after the Trojan War. At one point Ulysses recalls the end of the war, and tells the famous story of the wooden horse.

The same story of the horse appears in a book written many centuries later by a Roman poet. Virgil, born in 70 BC, wrote a book called the *Aeneid*. In it he claims that the Romans are the descendants of a warrior who fled from Troy after the destruction of the city by the Greeks.

People might well have come to Italy from the eastern Mediterranean countries at some point in history, but there is no historical connection at all between the Romans and the Trojans.

What the *Aeneid* does prove is that stories of the Trojan War were still popular over a thousand years after it had happened.

The hero of the *Aeneid,* Aeneas, tells how the siege of Troy was ended. One day the Trojans woke up and were amazed to find that the Greeks had disappeared. There was no enemy camp, and no fleet. The Trojans rejoiced.

Their joy soon gave way to puzzlement. For on the shore stood a huge horse made of wood. They hurried to their chariots and galloped over to the horse. What was it? Should they drag it into the city and find out?

The priest, Laocöon, warned the Trojans never to trust the Greeks. It was probably a trick, he said.

Just then some Trojan shepherds hurried to the scene. They had found a man with his hands tied. He was a Greek called Sinon. The Greeks, said Sinon, had gone away forever. They had built the horse as an offering to the goddess Athene. He was to have been a human sacrifice, but he had escaped. The horse, claimed Sinon, brought good fortune. The Greeks had made it so large that the Trojans would never be able to claim it for their city.

The fall of Troy

It was a trick, of course. The Greeks had not sailed away. Their fleet lay hidden behind an island called Tenedos. The horse was full of the best Greek warriors, armed to the teeth. In the *Odyssey* Ulysses tells of the fear he felt when he heard Laocöon's warning that the horse was a trap.

The Greeks had nothing to fear. The Trojans were completely taken in. They were determined to have this mighty offering to the gods inside their city. They even broke down part of the town walls, and hauled the heavy weight with ropes. It stuck no less than four times, but in their enthusiasm they never heard the clatter of weapons and armor from inside the horse's wooden body.

Eventually the horse stood inside the citadel of Troy. When night fell, the Greeks let themselves down on a rope from the belly of the horse. The Trojan sentires were killed silently. The city gates were opened: outside were the other Greek warriors, who had crept up under the cover of darkness.

The Trojans had been celebrating their victory. As they stumbled from their beds, they were met by a terrible sight: the Greeks in full battle array, and their beautiful city burning to the ground.

Troy was never forgotten. For thousands of years people told tales of the Trojan War. In the end nobody believed they were anything more than distant legends . . . until Heinrich Schliemann came to Hissarlik, determined to prove that Troy had once existed.

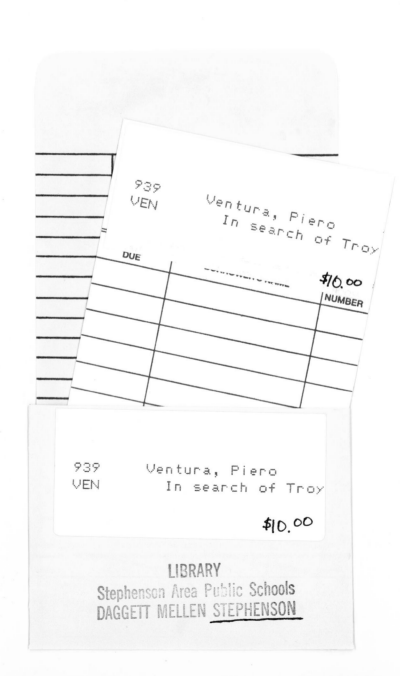